The Creation

Genesis 1, 2:1-3

Retold by Pamela Broughton
Illustrated by Robert Sentnor

A GOLDEN BOOK® • NEW YORK

In the beginning, God created the heavens and the earth.

At first, darkness was everywhere.

God said, "Let there be light." At once there was bright light. God moved the light apart from the darkness. He called the light day and the darkness night.

God saw that the light was good. There was evening and morning, the first day.

Then God made the sky, to divide the waters. There were waters above the sky, and waters below.

God saw that the sky was good. There was evening and morning, the second day.

God said, "Let all the waters under the sky be gathered into one place. Let the dry land appear."

It was so, and God called the dry land earth. The waters He called seas.

God saw that the earth and the seas were good.

God made plants and grasses to cover the land.
He made trees, with fruit hanging from the branches.
He made each growing thing to have seeds, that
more growing things like it might come to be.

God looked at what He had made, and He saw that it was good. And there was evening and morning, the third day.

And God said, "Let there be different lights in the sky, to serve as signs, to mark the days and the seasons and the years."

God made the sun to light the earth by day.

He made the moon to light the earth by night. He
made the stars as well.

God saw that it was good. And there was evening
and morning, the fourth day.

Then God said, "Let the seas be filled with living creatures." And He created great whales and little fishes and every creature that lives in the sea.

And God said, "Let birds fly through the sky." He created all the birds of the air, every creature that has wings. And they flew, and the sky was full of them.

God saw that all He had made was good. He blessed the living creatures that swim and fly. There was evening and morning, the fifth day.

Then God said, "Let there be living creatures to walk upon the earth."

God created cattle and creeping things and all the beasts that live on land. And God saw that it was good.

Then God created man and woman.

God said, "Let man and woman rule over the fishes of the sea, the birds of the sky, over all the earth and the beasts that live on it."

God blessed man and woman. He said, "Fill the earth with your children. Rule over the creatures of the sea, the birds of the air, and the beasts of the earth. See the grasses and plants and trees with fruit—these shall be for food for you and every living thing." And it was so.

God saw that everything He had made was very good. And there was evening and morning, the sixth day.

Then God rested from the work that He had done. And He blessed the seventh day, and made it a holy day of rest.